Cozy
for You &

Lion Brand® Homespun®

ade in America in a New Hampshire
ill that uses hydro-generated power,
on Brand® Homespun® has long
een a favorite of knitters and
ocheters. Lovely, lofty and quick to
it or crochet, Homespun® is available
dozens of beautifully blended
lorways, from heathery tweeds to
interly palettes, making even the
mplest of projects look absolutely
unning. Its bulky weight results in
fast finish for fashions and home
cessories, and its wash-and-wear
re makes Homespun® ideal for
most any project.

Lion Brand® Homespun® Thick & Quick®

Make a statement with Homespun® Thick & Quick®. This super-bulky version of fan-favorite Homespun® yarn works up quickly into richly textured afghans and silky-soft accessories such as hats, scarves and cowls. Made in an American mill in New Hampshire, this beautiful yarn features both heathers and slowly striping painterly shades, so you can easily find the color you love. This is sure to be your go-to yarn for quick-finish projects.

About Lion Brand® Yarn Company
Lion Brand® Yarn Company is a 5th generation, family-owned and operated business, and a beloved American brand since 1878. The company is devoted to inspiring and educating knitters and crocheters with yarns, patterns, how-tos, and ideas that elevate their yarn crafting experience.

LEISURE ARTS, INC.
Maumelle, Arkansas

Breezy Blue Shawl

◖■■☐▢ **EASY**

SIZE

About 20" x 65" (51 cm x 165 cm)

SHOPPING LIST

Yarn (Bulky Weight)

LION BRAND® HOMESPUN® (Art. #790)

- ☐ #404 Lagoon - 2 skeins (A)
- ☐ #368 Montana Sky - 1 skein (B)
- ☐ #341 Windsor - 1 skein (C)

  or colors of your choice

Crochet Hook

LION BRAND® crochet hook

- ☐ Size K-10.5 (6.5 mm)

  or size needed for gauge

Additional Supplies

- ☐ LION BRAND® large-eyed blunt needle

GAUGE

2 ripples = 13" (33 cm), measured from peak to peak.

BE SURE TO CHECK YOUR GAUGE.

NOTES

1. Shawl is worked in a ripple crochet pattern. The ripple pattern is easy to do, but it's important to remember that you may need to work several rows before the ripple pattern becomes clear.

2. The ripple pattern consists of alternating 3-st "peaks" and skipped st "valleys." Take care to keep the peaks and valleys of each row aligned. 3 Sts are worked into the center st of peaks, and sts are skipped over valleys.

3. When working in ripple crochet, your piece may not lie flat until you've worked a few rows.

4. To change color, work last st of old color to last yarn over. Yarn over with new color and draw through all loops on hook to complete the st. Fasten off old color. Proceed with new color.

STRIPE SEQUENCE

Work 4 rows with A, 2 rows with B, 2 rows with A, 2 rows with C, 2 rows with A, 2 rows with B, 2 rows with A, 2 rows with C, 2 rows with A, 2 rows with B, 4 rows with A.

SHAWL

With A, ch 162.

Row 1: Work 2 sc in 2nd ch from hook, *sc in next 5 ch, sk 1 ch, sc in next 9 ch, 3 sc in next ch, sc in next 9 ch, sk 1 ch, sc in next 5 ch**, 3 sc in next ch; rep from * 3 more times, then from * to **, 2 sc in last ch – 10 ripples at the end of this row.

Row 2: Ch 3 (does not count as
: in this row or in any of the
llowing rows), turn, work 2 dc
to first sc, *dc in next 5 sc, sk
sc, dc in next 9 sc, 3 dc in next sc,
: in next 9 sc, sk 2 sts, dc in next
sc **, 3 dc in next sc; rep from *
more times, then from * to **,
dc in last sc.

Row 3: Ch 1, turn, 2 sc in first dc,
sc in next 5 dc, sk 2 dc, sc in next
dc, 3 sc in next dc, sc in next
dc, sk 2 dc, sc in next 5 dc**,
sc in next dc; rep from * 3 more
mes, then from * to **, 2 sc in
st dc.

ep Rows 2 and 3, changing color
llowing Stripe Sequence, until
26 rows of Stripe Sequence
ive been worked.

sten off.

FINISHING
Bobbles (make 5)
With C, ch 4.

*Yarn over, insert hook in 4th ch
from hook, yarn over and draw
up a loop, yarn over and draw
through 2 loops on hook; rep from
* 6 times more in same ch, yarn
over, draw through all 8 loops on
hook, ch 1 and tighten, sl st in
base of bobble.

Fasten off, leaving a long yarn tail.
Use yarn tails to tie a Bobble to
the peak of each large ripple
along last row of Shawl.

Weave in ends.

Hearthside Ripple Afghan

EASY

SIZE

About 42" x 54" (106.5 cm x 137 cm)

SHOPPING LIST

Yarn (Bulky Weight)

LION BRAND® HOMESPUN® (Art. #790)

- ☐ #312 Edwardian - 2 skeins (A)
- ☐ #315 Tudor - 2 skeins (B)
- ☐ #407 Painted Desert - 2 skeins (C)

  or colors of your choice

Crochet Hook

LION BRAND® crochet hook

- ☐ Size K-10.5 (6.5 mm)

  or size needed for gauge

Additional Supplies

- ☐ LION BRAND® large-eyed blunt needle

GAUGE

1 ripple = about 6" (15 cm), measured from peak to peak.

BE SURE TO CHECK YOUR GAUGE.

STRIPE SEQUENCE

Work 6 rows with A, 2 rows with B, 4 rows with C, 2 rows with A, 4 rows with B, 6 rows with C, 4 rows with A, 6 rows with B, 6 rows with C, 2 rows with B, 2 rows with A, 2 rows with C, 4 rows with B, and 4 rows with A.

NOTES

1. This project is worked in a ripple crochet pattern. The ripple pattern is easy to do, but it's important to remember that you may need to work several rows before the ripple pattern becomes clear.

2. The ripple pattern consists of alternating 3-st "peaks" and skipped st "valleys." Take care t keep the peaks and valleys of each row aligned. 3 Sts are worked into the center st of peaks, and sts are skipped ove valleys.

3. When working in ripple crochet, your piece may not lie flat until you've worked a few rows.

4. To change color, work last st of old color to last yarn over Yarn over with new color and draw through all loops on hoo to complete the st. Fasten off old color. Proceed with new color.

AFGHAN

With A, ch 146.

Row 1: Work 2 sc in 2nd ch from hook, *sc in next 7 ch, sk next ch, sc in next 7 ch, 3 sc in next ch; rep from * to last 16 ch, sc in next 7 ch, sk next ch, sc in next 7 ch, 2 sc in last ch – 9 ripples.

Row 2: Ch 3 (counts as dc in this row and in all following rows), turn, dc in first sc, *dc in next 7 sc, sk next 2 sc, dc in next 7 sc, 3 dc in next sc; rep from * to last 17 sts, dc in next 7 sc, sk next 2 sc, dc in next sc, 2 dc in last sc.

Row 3: Ch 1, turn, 2 sc in first dc, sc in next 7 dc, sk next 2 dc, sc in next 7 dc, 3 sc in next dc; rep from * to last 17 sts, sc in next 7 dc, sk next 2 dc, sc in next 7 dc, 2 sc in top of turning ch.

Rep Rows 2 and 3, changing color following Stripe Sequence until all 54 rows of Stripe Sequence have been worked.

Fasten off.

FINISHING

Weave in ends.

Cozy Ripple Poncho

 **EASY**

SIZE

Finished Circumference: About 60" (152.5 cm), along lower edge.

Finished Length: About 20" (51 cm)

SHOPPING LIST

Yarn (Super Bulky Weight)

LION BRAND® HOMESPUN® THICK & QUICK® (Art. #792)

☐ #211 Granite Stripes - 2 skeins

  or color of your choice

Crochet Hook

LION BRAND® crochet hook

☐ size P-15 (10 mm)

  or size needed for gauge

Additional Supplies

☐ LION BRAND® large-eyed blunt needle

GAUGE

1 ripple at lower edge (with 7 sts between peaks and valleys)

= about 10" (25.5 cm).

4 rnds = about 5" (12.5 cm).

BE SURE TO CHECK YOUR GAUGE.

NOTES

1. Poncho is worked in joined rnds beg at lower edge. Turn at beg of each rnd.

2. Poncho is worked in a ripple crochet pattern. The ripple pattern consists of alternating 3-st "peaks" and skipped st "valleys." Take care to keep the peaks and valleys of each rnd aligned. 3 Sts are worked into the center st of peaks and sts are skipped over valleys. In Rnd 1 only 1 ch is skipped at a valley, so that there are no "holes" in the tips of the lower edge of Poncho. In all other rnds 2 sts are skipped at each valley.

3. Sts are decreased from lower edge up to neck edge. The total number of sts in a rnd is decreased by decreasing the number of sts between peaks and valleys.

4. When working in ripple crochet, your piece may not lie flat until you've worked a few rnds.

PONCHO

Loosely ch 96. Being careful not to twist ch; join with a sl st in first ch to form a ring.

Rnd 1: Ch 1, 2 sc in same ch as joining, *sc in next 7 ch, sk 1 ch, sc in next 7 ch, 3 sc in next ch; rep from * to last 15 ch, sc in next 7 ch sk 1 ch, sc in next 7 ch, sc again in same ch as joining; join with sl st in top of first sc – 6 ripples with 7 sc between peaks and valleys.

Rnds 2 and 3: Ch 3 (counts as first dc in this rnd and in all following rnds), turn, dc in same st as joining, *dc in next 7 sts, sk next 2 sts, dc in next 7 sts, 3 dc in next st; rep from * to last 16 sts, dc in next 7 sts, sk next 2 sts, dc in next 7 sts, dc again in same st as joining; join with sl st in top of beg ch.

Rnd 4 (Decrease Rnd): Ch 3, turn, dc in same st as joining, *sk next st, dc in next 6 sts, sk next 2 sts, dc in next 6 sts, sk next st, 3 dc in next st; rep from * to last 16 sts, sk next st, dc in next 6 sts, sk next 2 sts, dc in next 6 sts, sk next st, dc again in same st as joining; join with sl st in top of beg ch – 6 ripples with 6 dc between peaks and valleys.

Rnd 5: Ch 3, turn, dc in same st as joining, *dc in next 6 sts, sk next 2 sts, dc in next 6 sts, 3 dc in next st; rep from * to last 14 sts, dc in next 6 sts, sk next 2 sts, dc in next 6 sts, dc again in same st as joining; join with sl st in top of beg ch.

Rnd 6 (Decrease Rnd): Ch 3, turn, dc in same st as joining, *sk next st, dc in next 5 sts, sk next 2 sts, dc in next 5 sts, sk next st, 3 dc in next st; rep from * to last 14 sts, sk next st, dc in next 5 sts, sk next 2 sts, dc in next 5 sts, sk next st, dc again in same st as joining; join with sl st in top of beg ch – 6 ripples with 5 sts between peaks and valleys.

Rnd 7: Ch 3, turn, dc in same st as joining, *dc in next 5 sts, sk next 2 sts, dc in next 5 sts, 3 dc in next st; rep from * to last 12 sts, dc in next 5 sts, sk next 2 sts, dc in next 5 sts, dc again in same st as joining; join with sl st in top of beg ch.

Rnd 8 (Decrease Rnd): Ch 3, turn, dc in same st as joining, *sk next st, dc in next 4 sts, sk next 2 sts, dc in next 4 sts, sk next st, 3 dc in next st; rep from * to last 12 sts, sk next st, dc in next 4 sts, sk next 2 sts, dc in next 4 sts, sk next st, dc again in same st as joining; join with sl st in top of beg ch – 6 ripples with 4 sts between peaks and valleys.

Rnd 9: Ch 3, turn, dc in same st as joining, *dc in next 4 sts, sk next 2 sts, dc in next 4 sts, 3 dc in next st; rep from * to last 10 sts, dc in next 4 sts, sk next 2 sts, dc in next 4 sts, dc again in same st as joining; join with sl st in top of beg ch.

Rnd 10 (Decrease Rnd): Ch 3, turn, dc in same st as joining, *sk next st, dc in next 3 sts, sk next 2 sts, dc in next 3 sts, sk next st, 3 dc in next st; rep from * to last 10 sts, sk next st, dc in next 3 sts, sk next 2 sts, dc in next 3 sts, sk next st, dc again in same st as joining; join with sl st in top of beg ch – 6 ripples with 3 sts between peaks and valleys.

Rnd 11: Ch 3, turn, dc in same st as joining, *dc in next 3 sts, sk next 2 sts, dc in next 3 sts, 3 dc in next st; rep from * to last 8 sts, dc in next 3 sts, sk next 2 sts, dc in next 3 sts, dc again in same st as joining; join with sl st in top of beg ch.

Rnd 12 (Decrease Rnd): Ch 3, turn, dc in same st as joining, *sk next st, dc in next 2 sts, sk next 2 sts, dc in next 2 sts, sk next st, 3 dc in next st; rep from * to last 8 sts, sk next st, dc in next 2 sts, sk next 2 sts, dc in next 2 sts, sk next st, dc again in same st as joining; join with sl st in top of beg ch – 6 ripples with 2 sts between peaks and valleys.

Rnd 13: Ch 3, turn, dc in same st as joining, *dc in next 2 sts, sk next 2 sts, dc in next 2 sts, 3 dc in next st; rep from * to last 6 sts, dc in next 2 sts, sk next 2 sts, dc in next 2 sts, dc again in same st as joining; join with sl st in top of beg ch.

Rnds 14 and 15: Ch 1, turn, 2 sc in same st as joining, *sc in next 2 sts, sk next 2 sts, sc in next 2 sts, 3 sc in next st; rep from * to last 5 sts, sc in next 2 sts, sk next 2 sts, sc in next 2 sts, sc again in same st as joining; join with sl st in top of first sc.

Fasten off.

FINISHING
Weave in ends.

Graphic Ripple Afghan

■■□□ EASY

SIZE

About 45" x 56" (114.5 cm x 142 cm)

SHOPPING LIST

Yarn (Bulky Weight)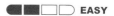

LION BRAND® HOMESPUN® (Art. #790)

- ☐ #368 Montana Sky - 1 skein (A)
- ☐ #373 Black - 3 skeins (B)
- ☐ #426 Tulips - 1 skein (C)
- ☐ #399 Apple Green - 1 skein (D)
- ☐ #386 Grape - 1 skein (E)
  - **or** colors of your choice

Crochet Hook

LION BRAND® crochet hook

- ☐ Size K-10.5 (6.5 mm)
  - **or** size needed for gauge

Additional Supplies

- ☐ LION BRAND® large-eyed blunt needle

GAUGE

1 ripple = about 5" (12.5 cm), measured from peak to peak.

10 sts + 5 rows = 4" (10 cm) in ripple pattern.

BE SURE TO CHECK YOUR GAUGE.

—— STITCH GUIDE ——

DOUBLE CROCHET 3 TOGETHER (abbreviated dc3tog) (uses 3 sts) (Yarn over, insert hook in next st and draw up a loop, yarn over, draw through 2 loops) 3 times, yarn over and draw through all 4 loops on hook – 2 sts decreased.

NOTES

1. This Afghan is worked in a ripple crochet pattern. The ripple pattern is easy to do, but it's important to remember that you may need to work several rows before the ripple pattern becomes clear.

2. The ripple in this design is created by working dc3tog to form "valleys" and 3 dc all in one st to form "peaks." In each row, take care to work dc3tog over the 3 sts in each "valley" and 3 dc in the center dc of each "peak."

3. When working in ripple crochet, your piece may not lie flat until you've worked a few rows.

4. To change color, work last st of old color to last yarn over. Yarn over with new color and draw through all loops on hook to complete the st. Fasten off old color. Proceed with new color.

STRIPE SEQUENCE

Work 10 rows each with A, B, C, B, D, B, and E.

AFGHAN

With A, ch 112.

Row 1: Dc in 4th ch from hook (beg ch counts as first dc), *dc in next 4 ch, dc3tog, dc in next 4 ch, 3 dc in next ch; rep from * 7 more times, dc in next 4 ch, dc3tog, dc in next 4 ch, 2 dc in last ch – 9 ripples.

Rows 2-10: Ch 3 (counts as first dc), turn, dc in first st, *dc in next 4 sts, dc3tog, dc in next 4 sts, 3 dc in next st; rep from * 7 more times, dc in next 4 sts, dc3tog, dc in next 4 sts, 2 dc in top of beg ch-3. Change to B in last st of Row 10.

Row 11: With B, ch 3 (counts as first dc), turn, working in back loops only, rep Row 2.

Rows 12-20: With B, rep Row 2. Change to C in last st of Row 20.

Rep Rows 11-20 continuing to change color every 10 rows following Stripe Sequence, until all 70 rows of Stripe Sequence have been completed.

Fasten off.

FINISHING

Weave in ends.

Ripple Mitts

■■□□ **EASY**

SIZE

Finished Circumference: About 9" (23 cm)

Finished Length: About 8½" (21.5 cm)

SHOPPING LIST

Yarn (Bulky Weight)

LION BRAND® HOMESPUN® (Art. #790)

☐ #381 Barley - 1 skein (A)

☐ #412 Pearls - 1 skein (B)

or colors of your choice

Crochet Hook

LION BRAND® crochet hook

☐ Size K-10.5 (6.5 mm)

or size needed for gauge

Additional Supplies

☐ LION BRAND® large-eyed blunt needle

GAUGE

1 ripple = about 3" (7.5 cm), measured from peak to peak.

BE SURE TO CHECK YOUR GAUGE.

NOTES

1. Mitts are worked in a ripple crochet pattern. The ripple pattern is easy to do, but it's important to remember that you may need to work several rows before the ripple pattern becomes clear.

2. The ripple pattern consists of alternating 3-st "peaks" and skipped st "valleys." Take care to keep the peaks and valleys of each row aligned. 3 Sts are worked into the center st of peaks, and sts are skipped over valleys.

3. When working in ripple crochet, your piece may not lie flat until you've worked a few rows.

4. Do not cut yarn between color changes, carry unused color along side edge of piece.

MITTS (make 2)

With A, ch 26.

Row 1: Sc in 2nd ch from hook, sc in next 2 ch, *3 sc in next ch, sc in next 3 ch, sk 2 ch, sc in next 3 ch; rep from * to last 4 ch, 3 sc in next ch, sc in next 3 ch – 27 sc (3 ripples with 3 sc between peaks and valleys) at the end of this row.

Row 2: With A, ch 1, turn, sk first sc, sc in next 3 sts, *3 sc in next st, sc in next 3 sts, sk 2 sts, sc in next 3 sts; rep from * to last 5 sts, 3 sc in next st, sc in next 2 sts, sk next sc, sc in last sc.

Change to B.

Rows 3 and 4: With B, rep Row 2.

Rows 5-8: With A, rep Row 2.

Rows 9-14: Rep Rows 3-8.

Row 15: With B, rep Row 2.

Fasten off.

FINISHING

From RS, join B with sl st at one end of Row 1. Ch 1, work sc evenly spaced across. Fasten off. Cut yarn, leaving a long yarn tail. Thread tail into blunt needle and sew sides of Mitt together for about 6" (15 cm). Leave next 2" (5 cm) open for thumb, then sew remainder of sides together.

Weave in ends.

Refreshing Ripple Afghan

■■□⊃ EASY

SIZE

About 42" x 52" (106.5 cm x 132 cm)

SHOPPING LIST

Yarn (Super Bulky Weight)

LION BRAND® HOMESPUN® THICK & QUICK® (Art. #792)

☐ #407 Painted Desert - 4 skeins (A)

☐ #404 Lagoon - 2 skeins (B)

   or colors of your choice

Crochet Hook

LION BRAND® crochet hook

☐ Size P-15 (10 mm)

   or size needed for gauge

Additional Supplies

☐ LION BRAND® large-eyed blunt needle

GAUGE

1 ripple = about 7" (18 cm), measured from peak to peak.

BE SURE TO CHECK YOUR GAUGE.

STRIPE SEQUENCE

Work 4 rows with A, *2 rows with B, 2 rows with A, 2 rows with B, 6 rows with A, 2 rows with B, 6 rows with A; rep from * once more, then 2 rows with B, 2 rows with A, 2 rows with B and 4 rows with A.

NOTES

1. Afghan is worked in a ripple crochet pattern. The ripple pattern is easy to do, but it's important to remember that you may need to work several rows before the ripple pattern becomes clear.

2. The ripple pattern consists of alternating 3-st "peaks" and skipped st "valleys." Take care to keep the peaks and valleys of each row aligned. 3 Sts are worked into the center st of peaks, and sts are skipped over valleys.

3. When working in ripple crochet, your piece may not lie flat until you've worked a few rows.

4. To change color, work last st of old color to last yarn over. Yarn over with new color and draw through all loops on hook to complete the st. Fasten off old color. Proceed with new color.

AFGHAN

With A, ch 70.

Row 1: Hdc in 3rd ch from hook
(2 skipped ch count as first hdc),
hdc in next 4 ch, *3 hdc in next
ch, hdc in next 5 ch, sk next ch,
hdc in next ch, sk next ch, hdc in
next 5 ch; rep from * to last 7 ch,
[?] hdc in next ch, hdc in last 6 ch –
[?] ripples at the end of this row.

Row 2: Ch 2 (counts as first hdc),
turn, sk first 2 hdc, hdc in next
[?] hdc, *3 hdc in next hdc (center
[?] of previous "peak"), hdc in next
[?] hdc, sk next hdc, hdc in next
hdc, sk next hdc, hdc in next
[?] hdc; rep from * to last 8 hdc
[?] hdc and ch-2), 3 hdc in next
[?] dc, hdc in next 5 hdc, sk next
[?] dc, hdc in top of beg ch.

Rep Row 2, changing color
following Stripe Sequence until all
54 rows of Stripe Sequence have
been worked.

Fasten off.

FINISHING

Weave in ends.

Bobble Ripple Cowl

EASY

SIZE

Finished Circumference: About 32" (81 cm)

Finished Height: About 9" (23 cm)

SHOPPING LIST

Yarn (Bulky Weight)

LION BRAND® HOMESPUN® (Art. #790)

- ☐ # 426 Tulips - 1 skein

  or color of your choice

Crochet Hook

LION BRAND® crochet hook

- ☐ Size K-10.5 (6.5 mm)

  or size needed for gauge

Additional Supplies

- ☐ LION BRAND® large-eyed blunt needle

GAUGE

1 ripple = 4" (10 cm), measured from peak to peak.

BE SURE TO CHECK YOUR GAUGE.

—— STITCH GUIDE ——

BOBBLE (worked all in one stitch) Yarn over, insert hook in indicated st and draw up a loop, yarn over and draw through 2 loops on hook (2 loops rem on hook), *yarn over, insert hook in **same** st and draw up a loop, yarn over and draw through 2 loops on hook; rep from * once **more**, yarn over and draw through all 4 loops on hook.

NOTES

1. Cowl is worked in joined rnds beg at lower edge. Turn at beg of each rnd.
2. Cowl is worked in a ripple crochet pattern. The ripple pattern consists of alternating 3-st "peaks" and skipped st "valleys." Take care to keep the peaks and valleys of each rnd aligned. 3 Sts are worked into the center st of peaks, and sts are skipped over valleys.
3. The ripple pattern is easy to do, but it's important to remember that you may need to work several rnds before the ripple pattern becomes clear.
4. When working in ripple crochet, your piece may not lie flat until you've worked a few rnds.

COWL

Loosely ch 104. Being careful not to twist ch; join with sl st in first ch to form a ring.

Rnd 1: Ch 1, 2 sc in same ch as joining, *sc in next 5 ch, sk 2 ch, sc in next 5 ch, 3 sc in next ch; rep from * to last 12 ch, sc in next 5 ch, sk 2 ch, sc in next 5 ch, sc again in same ch as first sc; join with sl st in first sc – 104 sc (8 ripples with 5 sts between peaks and valleys) at the end of this rnd.

nd 2 (WS): Ch 3, turn, (yarn over, insert hook in **same** st as joining nd draw up a loop, yarn over and raw through 2 loops on hook) wice, yarn over and draw through ll 3 loops on hook (first bobble nade), sc in same st as joining, sc in next 5 sts, sk 2 sts, sc in next sts, (sc, bobble, sc) in next st; ep from * to last 12 sts, sc in next sts, sk 2 sts, sc in next 5 sts, sc in ame st as joining; join with sl st in op of bobble.

nd 3: Ch 1, turn, 2 sc in same t as joining, *sc in next 5 sts, sk sts, sc in next 5 sts, 3 sc in next st op of bobble); rep from * to last 2 sts, sc in next 5 sts, sk 2 sts, sc n next 5 sts, sc in same st as first c; join with sl st in first sc.

Rnds 4 and 5: Ch 1, turn, 2 sc in same st as joining, *sc in next 5 sts, sk 2 sts, sc in next 5 sts, 3 sc in next st; rep from * to last 12 sts, sc in next 5 sts, sk 2 sts, sc in next 5 sts, sc in same st as first sc; join with sl st in first sc.

Rnds 6-13: Rep Rnds 2-5 twice.

Rnds 14 and 15: Rep Rnds 2 and 3.

Rnd 16: Rep Rnd 2.

Fasten off.

FINISHING
Weave in ends.

Eyelet Ripple Afghan

EASY

SIZE
About 46" x 56" (117 cm x 142 cm)

SHOPPING LIST

Yarn (Super Bulky Weight)

LION BRAND® HOMESPUN® THICK & QUICK® (Art. #792)

- ☐ #201 Coral Stripes - 5 skeins

  or color of your choice

Crochet Hook

LION BRAND® crochet hook

- ☐ Size P-15 (10 mm)

  or size needed for gauge

Additional Supplies

- ☐ LION BRAND® large-eyed blunt needle

GAUGE

1 ripple = about 6½" (16.5 cm), measured from peak to peak.

BE SURE TO CHECK YOUR GAUGE.

— STITCH GUIDE —

CLUSTER (abbreviated Cl)

[Y]arn over, insert hook in indicated [s]t and draw up a loop, yarn over [a]nd draw through 2 loops on [h]ook (2 loops rem on hook), *yarn [o]ver, insert hook in **same** st and [d]raw up a loop, yarn over and [d]raw through 2 loops on hook; [re]p from * 3 more times (6 loops [r]em on hook), yarn over and draw [t]hrough all loops on hook.

NOTES

1. Afghan is worked in a ripple crochet pattern. The ripple pattern is easy to do, but it's important to remember that you may need to work several rows before the ripple pattern becomes clear.

2. The ripple pattern consists of alternating ch-2 or (dc, ch 1, Cl, ch 1, dc) "peaks" and skipped st "valleys." Take care to keep the peaks and valleys of each row aligned. You may wish to use stitch markers to mark each peak.
3. When working in ripple crochet, your piece may not lie flat until you've worked a few rows.

AFGHAN

Ch 84.

Row 1: Dc in 4th ch from hook (beg ch counts as first dc), dc in next 3 ch, *ch 2, dc in next 5 ch, sk next 2 ch, dc in next 5 ch; rep from * to last 5 ch, ch 2, dc in last 5 ch – 7 ripples.

Row 2: Ch 3 (counts as first dc), turn, sk first 2 dc, dc in next 3 dc, *(dc, ch 1, Cl, ch 1, dc) in next ch-2 sp, dc in next 4 dc, sk next 2 dc, dc in next 4 dc; rep from * to last ch-2 sp, (dc, ch 1, Cl, ch 1, dc) in last ch-2 sp, dc in next 3 dc, sk next dc, dc in top of beg ch.

Row 3: Ch 3 (counts as first dc), turn, sk first 2 dc, dc in next 3 dc, dc in next ch-1 sp, *ch 2, dc in next ch-1 sp, dc in next 4 dc, sk next 2 dc, dc in next 4 dc, dc in next ch-1 sp; rep from * to last ch-1 sp, ch 2, dc in last ch-1 sp, dc in next 3 dc, sk next dc, dc in top of beg ch.

Rep Rows 2 and 3 until piece measures about 56" (142 cm) from beg.

Fasten off.

FINISHING

Weave in ends.

Ripple Triangle Afghan

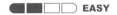 **EASY**

SIZE

About 50" x 50" (127 cm x 127 cm)

Shown on page 39.

SHOPPING LIST

Yarn (Super Bulky Weight)

LION BRAND® HOMESPUN® THICK & QUICK® (Art. #792)

☐ #211 Granite Stripes - 5 skeins

   or color of your choice

Crochet Hook

LION BRAND® crochet hook

☐ Size P-15 (10 mm)

   or size needed for gauge

Additional Supplies

☐ LION BRAND® large-eyed blunt needle

GAUGE

7 sts + 5 rows = about 4" (10 cm) in ripple pattern.

One Triangle = about 50" (127 cm) wide at base x 25" (63.5 cm) tall.

BE SURE TO CHECK YOUR GAUGE.

— STITCH GUIDE —

SINGLE CROCHET 2 TOGETHER
(abbreviated sc2tog) (uses 2 sts)
(Insert hook in next st and draw
up a loop) twice, yarn over and
draw through all 3 loops on hook
– 1 st decreased.

SINGLE CROCHET 3 TOGETHER
(abbreviated sc3tog) (uses 3 sts)
(Insert hook in next st and draw
up a loop) 3 times, yarn over and
draw through all 4 loops on hook
– 2 sts decreased.

SINGLE CROCHET 4 TOGETHER
(abbreviated sc4tog) (uses 4 sts)
(Insert hook in next st and draw
up a loop) 4 times, yarn over and
draw through all 5 loops on hook
– 3 sts decreased.

SINGLE CROCHET 5 TOGETHER
(abbreviated sc5tog) (uses 5 sts)
(Insert hook in next st and draw
up a loop) 5 times, yarn over and
draw through all 6 loops on hook
– 4 sts decreased.

NOTES

1. Afghan is made from
   4 Triangles sewn together to
   form a square.
2. Each Triangle is worked in
   a ripple crochet pattern,
   beginning at widest edge
   (base). Decreases are worked
   at each end of each row to
   shape sides of Triangle.

TRIANGLE (make 4)

Ch 92.

Row 1 (WS): Sc in 2nd ch from
hook and in each ch across –
91 sc.

Row 2 (RS): Ch 1, turn, sc3tog,
*sc in next st, (ch 1, sc in next st)
4 times, sc5tog; rep from * to last
8 sts, sc in next st, (ch 1, sc in next
st) 4 times, sc3tog – 9 ripples.

Row 3: Ch 1, turn, sc2tog, sc in
each sc and ch-1 sp to last 2 sts,
sc2tog – 89 sc.

Row 4: Ch 1, turn, sc3tog, sc in next 2 sts, (ch 1, sc in next st) twice, sc5tog, *sc in next st, (ch 1, sc in next st) 4 times, sc5tog; rep from * to last 7 sts, sc in next 2 sts, (ch 1, sc in next sc) twice, sc3tog – 85 sts (counting each sc and ch-1 sp as 1 st).

Row 5: Rep Row 3 – 83 sc.

Row 6: Ch 1, turn, sc2tog, sc in next st, ch 1, sc in next st, sc5tog, *sc in next st, (ch 1, sc in next st) 4 times, sc5tog; rep from * to last 4 sts, sc in next st, ch 1, sc in next st, sc2tog – 79 sts.

Row 7: Rep Row 3 – 77 sc.

Row 8: Ch 1, turn, sc in first st, sc5tog, *sc in next st, (ch 1, sc in next st) 4 times, sc5tog; rep from * to last st, sc in last st – 73 sts (about 7 ripples).

Row 9: Rep Row 3 – 71 sc.

Row 10: Ch 1, turn, sc4tog, sc in next st, (ch 1, sc in next st) 3 time sc5tog, *sc in next st, (ch 1, sc in next st) 4 times, sc5tog; rep from to last 8 sts, sc in next st, (ch 1, sc in next st) 3 times, sc4tog – 67 sts

Row 11: Rep Row 3 – 65 sc.

Row 12: Ch 1, turn, sc2tog, sc in next 2 sts, ch 1, sc in next st, sc5tog, *sc in next st, (ch 1, sc in next st) 4 times, sc5tog; rep from to last 5 sts, sc in next st, ch 1, sc i next 2 sts, sc2tog – 61 sts.

Row 13: Rep Row 3 – 59 sc.

Row 14: Ch 1, turn, sc in first 2 sts sc5tog, *sc in next st, (ch 1, sc in next st) 4 times, sc5tog; rep from to last 2 sts, sc in last 2 sts – 55 sts (about 5 ripples).

Row 15: Rep Row 3 – 53 sc.

Row 16: Ch 1, turn, sc4tog, sc in next 2 sts, (ch 1, sc in next st) 3 times, sc5tog, *sc in next st, (ch 1, sc in next st) 4 times, sc5tog; rep from * to last 9 sts, sc in next 2 sts, (sc in next st, ch 1) 3 times, sc4tog – 49 sts.

Row 17: Rep Row 3 – 47 sc.

Row 18: Ch 1, turn, sc3tog, sc in next st, (ch 1, sc in next st) twice, sc5tog, *sc in next st, (ch 1, sc in next st) 4 times, sc5tog; rep from * to last 6 sts, sc in next st, (ch 1, sc in next st) twice, sc3tog – 43 sts.

Row 19: Rep Row 3 – 41 sc.

Row 20: Ch 1, turn, sc in first 3 sts, sc5tog, *sc in next st, (ch 1, sc in next st) 4 times, sc5tog; rep from * to last 3 sts, sc in last 3 sts – 37 sts.

Row 21: Rep Row 3 – 35 sc.

Row 22: Ch 1, turn, sc5tog, *sc in next st, (ch 1, sc in next st) 4 times, sc5tog; rep from * across – 31 sts (3 ripples).

Rows 23-29: Rep Rows 3-9 – 11 sc at the end of Row 29.

Row 30: Ch 1, turn, sc4tog, sc in next sc, (ch 1, sc in next st) twice, sc4tog – 7 sts.

Row 31: Rep Row 3 – 5 sc.

Row 32: Ch 1, turn, sc5tog – 1 st.

Fasten off.

FINISHING

Sew Triangles tog to form a square, with tips of Triangles meeting at center of square.

Weave in ends.

Buttoned Wrap

■■□□ **EASY**

SIZE

Finished Circumference at Lower Edge: About 116" (294.5 cm)

Finished Length: About 26" (66 cm)

SHOPPING LIST

Yarn (Bulky Weight)

LION BRAND® HOMESPUN® (Art. #790)

☐ #381 Barley - 3 skeins

or color of your choice

Crochet Hook

LION BRAND® crochet hook

☐ Size K-10.5 (6.5 mm)

or size needed for gauge

Additional Supplies

☐ LION BRAND® large-eyed blunt needle

☐ One button 1" (25 mm) diameter

GAUGE

8 dc + 4 rows = 4" (10 cm).

BE SURE TO CHECK YOUR GAUGE.

——— STITCH GUIDE ———

DOUBLE CROCHET 2 TOGETHER (abbreviated dc2tog) (uses 2 sts) (Yarn over, insert hook in next st and draw up a loop, yarn over and draw through 2 loops) twice, yarn over and draw through all 3 loops on hook – 1 st decreased.

NOTE
Wrap is worked in one piece from lower edge to top and shaped with decreases.

WRAP

Loosely ch 329.

Row 1: Sc in 2nd ch from hook, sc in each of next 19 ch, *sk next ch, sc in next 40 ch; rep from * 6 more times, sk next ch, sc in last 20 ch – 320 sc.

Row 2: Ch 3 (counts as first dc in this row and in all following rows turn, dc in next 18 sts, *sk next 2 sts, dc in next 38 sts; rep from * 6 more times, sk next 2 sts, dc in last 19 sts – 304 dc at the end of this row.

Row 3: Ch 3, turn, dc in next 15 st dc2tog, *sk next 2 sts, dc in next 17 sts, dc2tog, dc in next 17 sts; re from * 6 more times, sk next 2 sts dc2tog, dc in last 16 sts – 279 dc.

Row 4: Ch 3, turn, dc in next 13 st dc2tog, *sk next 2 sts, dc2tog, dc in next 14 sts, dc2tog, dc in next 13 sts, dc2tog; rep from * 6 more times, sk next 2 sts, dc2tog, dc in next 14 sts – 240 dc.

Row 5: Ch 3, turn, dc in next 11 sts, dc2tog, *sk next 2 sts, dc2tog, dc in next 10 sts, (dc2tog) twice, dc in next 10 sts, dc2tog; rep from * 6 more times, sk next 2 sts, dc2tog, dc in last 12 sts – 94 sts.

Row 6: Ch 3, turn, dc in next 9 sts, dc2tog, *sk next 2 sts, dc2tog, dc in next 7 sts, (dc2tog) twice, dc in next 7 sts, dc2tog, sk next 2 sts, dc2tog, dc in next 18 sts, dc2tog; rep from * 2 more times, sk next 2 sts, dc2tog, dc in next 7 sts, (dc2tog) twice, dc in next 7 sts, dc2tog, sk next 2 sts, dc2tog, dc in next 10 sts – 154 sts.

Row 7: Ch 3, turn, dc in next 17 sts, *(dc2tog) twice, dc in next 34 sts; rep from * 2 more times, (dc2tog) twice, dc in last 18 sts – 146 sts.

Row 8: Ch 3, turn, dc in next 16 sts, *(dc2tog) twice, dc in next 32 sts; rep from * 2 more times, (dc2tog) twice, dc in last 17 sts – 138 sts.

Row 9: Ch 3, turn, dc in next 15 sts, *(dc2tog) twice, dc in next 30 sts; rep from * 2 more times, (dc2tog) twice, dc in last 16 sts – 130 sts.

Row 10: Ch 3, turn, dc in next 14 sts, *(dc2tog) twice, dc in next 28 sts; rep from * 2 more times, (dc2tog) twice, dc in last 15 sts – 122 sts.

Row 11: Ch 3, turn, dc in next 13 sts, *(dc2tog) twice, dc in next 26 sts; rep from * 2 more times, (dc2tog) twice, dc in last 14 sts – 114 sts.

Row 12: Ch 3, turn, dc in next 12 sts, *(dc2tog) twice, dc in next 24 sts; rep from * 2 more times, (dc2tog) twice, dc in last 13 sts – 106 sts.

Row 13: Ch 3, turn, dc in next 11 sts, *(dc2tog) twice, dc in next 22 sts; rep from * 2 more times, (dc2tog) twice, dc in last 12 sts – 98 sts.

Row 14: Ch 3, turn, dc in next 10 sts, *(dc2tog) twice, dc in next 20 sts; rep from * 2 more times, (dc2tog) twice, dc in last 11 sts – 90 sts.

Row 15: Ch 3, turn, dc in next 9 sts, *(dc2tog) twice, dc in next 18 sts; rep from * 2 more times, (dc2tog) twice, dc in last 10 sts – 82 sts.

Rows 16, 18, 20 and 22: Ch 3, turn, dc in each st across.

Row 17: Ch 3, turn, dc in next 8 sts, *(dc2tog) twice, dc in next 16 sts; rep from * 2 more times, (dc2tog) twice, dc in last 9 sts – 74 sts.

Row 19: Ch 3, turn, dc in next 7 sts, *(dc2tog) twice, dc in next 14 sts; rep from * 2 more times, (dc2tog) twice, dc in last 8 sts – 66 sts.

Row 21: Ch 3, turn, dc in next 6 sts, *(dc2tog) twice, dc in next 12 sts; rep from * 2 more times, (dc2tog) twice, dc in last 7 sts – 58 sts.

ow 23: Ch 3, turn, dc in next
sts, *(dc2tog) twice, dc in next
0 sts; rep from * 2 more times,
dc2tog) twice, dc in last 6 sts –
0 sts.

ows 24-26: Ch 3, turn, dc in each
t across.

asten off.

FINISHING

Sew button to left front, about
5" (12.5 cm) below top edge. Use
space between stitches on right
front for buttonhole.

Weave in ends.

General Instructions

ABBREVIATIONS

beg = begin(ning)(s)

ch = chain

ch-sp(s) = chain space previously
made

cm = centimeter

dc = double crochet

hdc = half double crochet

mm = millimeters

rem = remain(ing)(s)

rep = repeat

RS = right side

rnd(s) = round(s)

sc = single crochet

sk = skip

sl st = slip stitch

sp(s) = space(s)

st(s) = stitch(es)

tog = together

WS = wrong side

* — When you see an asterisk used within a pattern row or round, the symbol indicates that later you will be told to repeat a portion of the instruction. Most often the instructions will say, repeat from * so many times.

( ) or [ ] — Sets off a short numbe of stitches that are repeated **or** indicates additional information.

— When you see – (dash) followe by a number of stitches, this tells you how many stitches you will have at the end of a row or round

GAUGE

Never underestimate the importance of gauge. Achieving the correct gauge assures that the finished size of your piece matches the finished size given in the pattern.

CROCHET HOOKS

U.S.	B-1	C-2	D-3	E-4	F-5	G-6	H-8	I-9	J-10	K-10½	L-11	M/N-13	N/P-15	P/Q	Q	S
Metric - mm	2.25	2.75	3.25	3.5	3.75	4	5	5.5	6	6.5	8	9	10	15	16	19

CROCHET TERMINOLOGY

UNITED STATES		INTERNATIONAL
slip stitch (slip st)	=	single crochet (sc)
single crochet (sc)	=	double crochet (dc)
half double crochet (hdc)	=	half treble crochet (htr)
double crochet (dc)	=	treble crochet (tr)
treble crochet (tr)	=	double treble crochet (dtr)
double treble crochet (dtr)	=	triple treble crochet (ttr)
triple treble crochet (tr tr)	=	quadruple treble crochet (qtr)
skip	=	miss

Yarn Weight Symbol & Names	LACE 0	SUPER FINE 1	FINE 2	LIGHT 3	MEDIUM 4	BULKY 5	SUPER BULKY 6
Type of Yarns in Category	Fingering, 10-count crochet thread	Sock, Fingering Baby	Sport, Baby	DK, Light Worsted	Worsted, Afghan, Aran	Chunky, Craft, Rug	Bulky, Roving
Crochet Gauge* Ranges in Single Crochet to 4" (10 cm)	32-42 double crochets**	21-32 sts	16-20 sts	12-17 sts	11-14 sts	8-11 sts	5-9 sts
Advised Hook Size Range	Steel*** 6,7,8 Regular hook B-1	B-1 to E-4	E-4 to 7	7 to I-9	I-9 to K-10½	K-10½ to M/N-13	M/N-13 and larger

*GUIDELINES ONLY: The chart above reflects the most commonly used gauges and hook sizes for specific yarn categories.

** Lace weight yarns are usually crocheted on larger-size hooks to create lacy openwork patterns. Accordingly, a gauge range is difficult to determine. Always follow the gauge stated in your pattern.

*** Steel crochet hooks are sized differently from regular hooks–the higher the number the smaller the hook, which is the reverse of regular hook sizing.

■□□□ BEGINNER	Projects for first-time crocheters using basic stitches. Minimal shaping.
■■□□ EASY	Projects using yarn with basic stitches, repetitive stitch patterns, simple color changes, and simple shaping and finishing.
■■■□ INTERMEDIATE	Projects using a variety of techniques, such as basic lace patterns or color patterns, mid-level shaping and finishing.
■■■■ EXPERIENCED	Projects with intricate stitch patterns, techniques and dimension, such as non-repeating patterns, multi-color techniques, fine threads, small hooks, detailed shaping and refined finishing.

CHECKING YOUR GAUGE

Work a swatch that is at least 4" (10 cm) square. Use the suggested hook size and the number of stitches given. If your swatch is larger than 4" (10 cm), you need to work it again using a smaller hook; if it is smaller than 4" (10 cm), try it with a larger hook. This might require a swatch or two to get the exact gauge given in the pattern.

METRICS

As a handy reference, keep in mind that 1 ounce = approximately 28 grams and 1" = 2.5 centimeters.

TERMS

fasten off — To end your piece, you need to simply cut and pull the yarn through the last loop left on the hook. This keeps the last stitch intact and prevents the work from unraveling.

right side — Refers to the front or "public" side of the piece.

VISIT LionBrand.com FOR:
- Learn to Knit & Crochet Instructions
- Weekly newsletter with articles, tips, and updates
- Store Locator